SOCKS

Douglas Hill

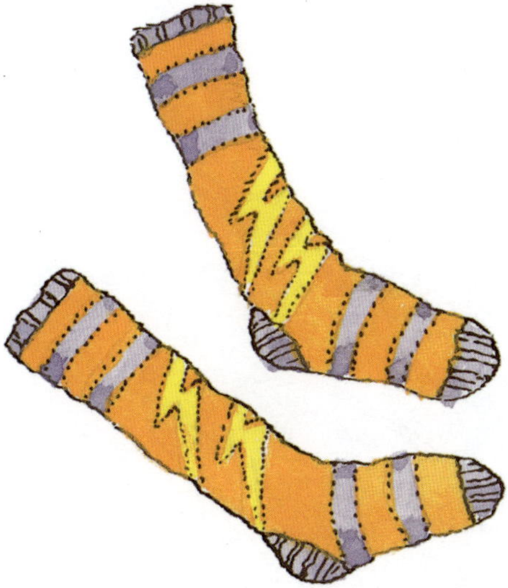

Illustrated by
Chris Fisher

OXFORD
UNIVERSITY PRESS

It was the morning after Rob's birthday. His Gran said, "Are you going to wear your new socks?"

The socks were bright orange, with purple stripes and yellow zigzags. Gran was always knitting things for him. Scarves, jumpers, hats, socks – they were all wild colours and crazy patterns.

"Do I have to?" Rob asked.

"Don't upset your Gran!" his mum told him.

"Put them on," Gran said, smiling. "See what happens."

Rob knew what would happen. The other children at school would laugh at him. Rob got laughed at a lot, most of all when he played football.

Rob loved football, but he wasn't good at it. When he got the ball, he often fell over. And he could never kick it straight.

He went to put on the socks. They made his feet tingle, as if the colours were hot. But Rob was too cross to care.

At school, everyone laughed at him.

"Nice socks, Rob!" one of them teased. Rob made a face.

"I had to wear them," he mumbled.

After school, Rob and the other children went to the football pitch. The school team was training with the PE teacher, Mr Teed.

As Rob watched, one of the team kicked the ball too far. It flew towards Rob and landed at his feet.

“Give us the ball!” shouted Big Jon, the team captain.

“Kick it, Rob,” said Mr Teed.

“If you can’t kick it,” yelled Stanley, the goalkeeper, “pick it up and carry it!”

Everyone laughed.

Rob went red. He hardly noticed that Gran's socks were tingling again. He poked at the football with one foot. The tingling grew stronger.

Suddenly he was running, fast and light-footed. AND he was keeping the ball at his feet!

The other children stared in silence, mouths open.

Big Jon rushed at him. He swung a leg in a wild tackle. But Rob skipped past him, and Jon's boot missed.

Rob ran faster, still with the ball. The rest of the team tried to tackle him. But he dodged and did a zigzag past them all.

At last there was only Stanley, the goalkeeper. Rob shot, hard and straight. The ball flew into the top corner of the goal.

Stanley landed face down in a puddle.

All the children gave a tremendous cheer. Big Jon stared at Rob.

"How did you get to be a star?" he asked.

"Yes, Rob," said Mr Teed. "When did you get so good at football?"

"I don't know," Rob said. "It just happened."

Mr Teed smiled. “You’d better start training with the school team. We need someone as good as you.” Rob smiled a huge happy smile. But he also had an odd idea.

When Rob got home, he took off Gran's socks and put on a different pair. Then he took a ball into the garden.

It was just like before. He couldn't kick it straight, or hard. When he tried to run with it, he fell over.

Then he put Gran's socks on again. He was just as good with the ball as he had been at school. Rob rushed inside to find Gran.

"I'm on the school team! Because of your socks! " he told her. "Are they magic?"

Gran put a finger to her lips.

"Don't tell anyone. Not even your mum and dad."

Then Rob had a scary thought. "How long will the socks last?" he asked.

"Years," Gran said. "But when you're older and bigger you might not need them anymore. Maybe then you'll be good at football all by yourself."

She smiled, and went back to her knitting.